This book belongs to:

_____

_____

Nature

Nature

ALAIN GRÉE

Button
BOOKS

First published 2012 by Button Books, an imprint of Guild of Master
Craftsman Publications Ltd, Castle Place, 166 High Street, Lewes,
East Sussex BN7 1XU.
Text © GMC Publications Ltd, 2012 Copyright in the Work ©
GMC Publications Ltd, 2012 Illustrations © 2012 A.G. & RicoBel.
ISBN 978 1 90898 505 7

Publisher: Jonathan Bailey; Production Manager: Jim Bulley; Managing
Editor: Gerrie Purcell; Senior Project Editor: Dominique Page; Managing
Art Editor: Gilda Pacitti; Colour origination by GMC Reprographics;
Printed and bound in China by Leo Paper Products.

On the farm

Can you find these animals on the farm?

cow

duck

pig

goat

sheep

hen

The cow gives us...

milk, butter, cheese
and beef

Did you know that most
of the food we eat comes
from the farm?

The pig gives us...

The hen gives us...

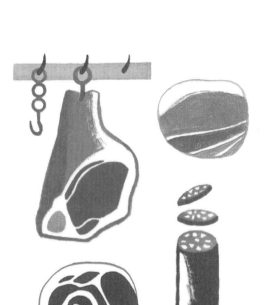

pork, bacon,
ham and sausages

eggs and chicken

In the fields, the farmer
grows crops such as corn,
wheat, fruit and vegetables.

When everything is ready, it is taken away on a tractor.

The wheat is turned into flour, which is used to make bread, biscuits and cakes.

The fruit and vegetables are sold in the shops for us to eat.

14

The farmer has grown lots of fruit and vegetables on the farm. The children are helping to pick them.

How many types of fruit and vegetable can you name?

15

In the forest

The forest is full of trees and plants.

chestnut tree

pine tree

oak tree

fern

holly

mistletoe

From forests we get wood, which can
be made into many useful things.

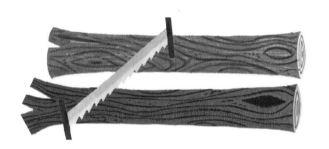 

First, the trees are chopped down and cut into logs.

A lorry takes the logs to a mill.

At the mill the logs are cut into planks of wood.

 A carpenter can turn the wood into furniture, such as tables and chairs.

Can you find these forest animals in the picture on the left?

pheasant

rabbit

wolf

fox

owl

Can you find these animals in the picture on the right?

snail

mouse

woodpecker

squirrel

deer

bird

wild boar

turtle

In the garden

flower

garden fork

watering can and hose

greenhouse

24

Lots of birds and animals like to visit the garden.

fox

hedgehog

frog

snail

blue tit

swallow

jay

robin

pigeon

sparrow

raven

In the garden we grow pretty flowers. The children like to pick them to give to mummy, or to press flat and make a picture with.

tulip

daffodil

Bees love the brightly coloured flowers. They collect pollen from them to make into honey.

Buzzzz...

We like to grow fruit and vegetables in our garden.
First, we dig the soil and sow the seeds.

The seeds need water and sunshine to make them grow.

When they are big enough, we can pick the fruit and vegetables and eat them.

Insects

butterfly

bees

dragonfly

fly

caterpillar

ladybird

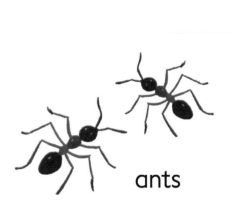

ants

In the meadow

Can you find these flowers in the meadow?

poppy

cornflower

dandelion

buttercup

daisy

Let's go for a walk in the meadow.
What might we find?

We found...

flowers

a feather

blackberries

mushrooms

At the seaside

At the seaside, there
are lots of birds, shells
and fish to discover.

Birds that live by the sea

guillemot

penguin

seagull

puffin

pelican

cormorant

What can we see in a rockpool?

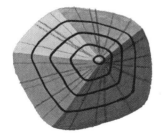

barnacle

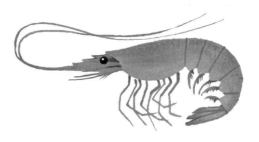

shrimp

starfish

shells

seaweed

mussel

Who lives under the sea?

lobster

octopus

crab

hermit crab

43

Some of the fish in the sea

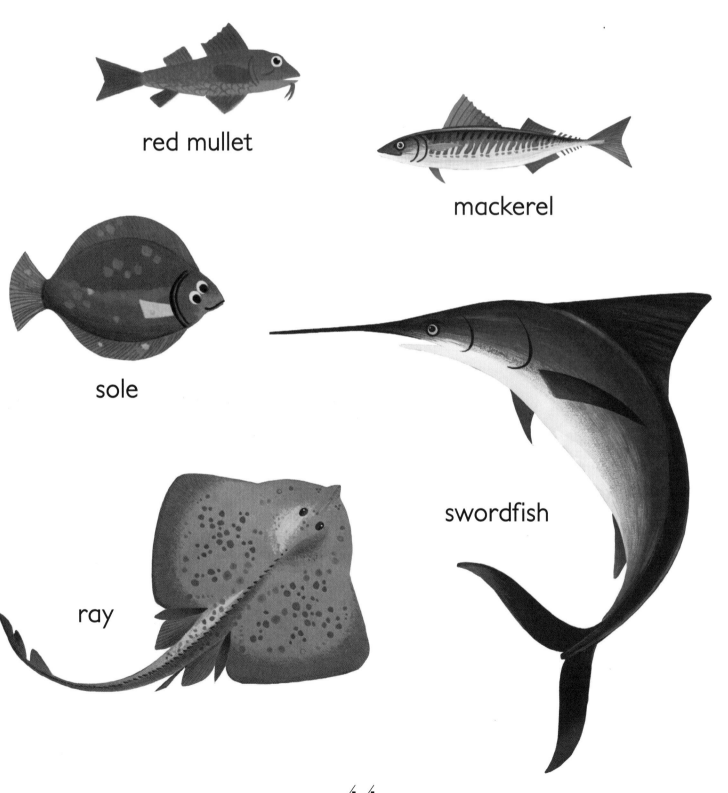

red mullet

mackerel

sole

ray

swordfish

44

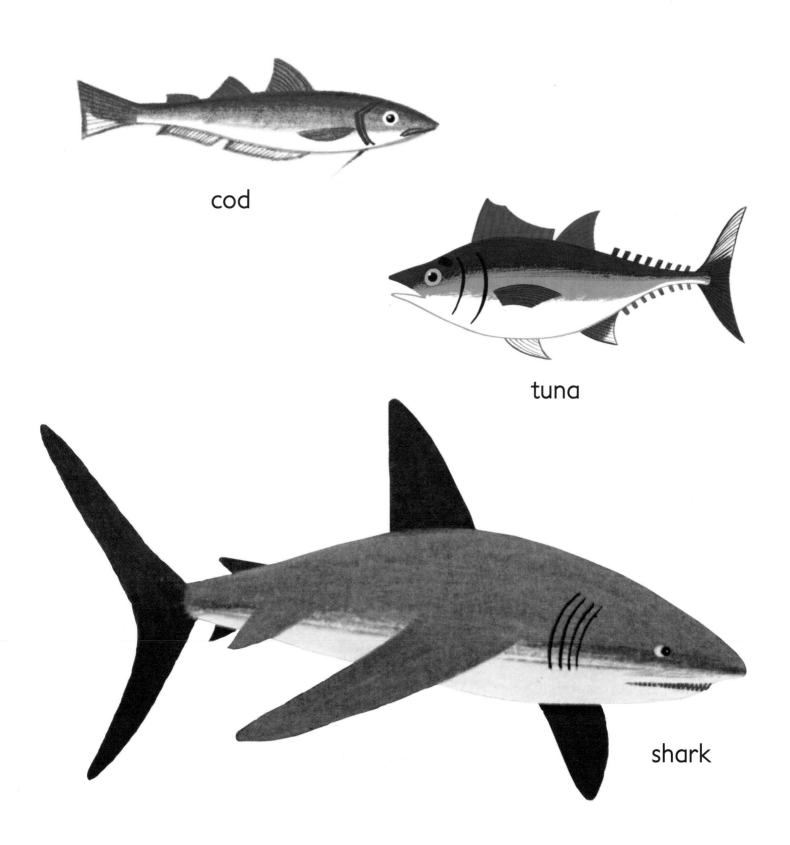

cod

tuna

shark

But by far the biggest creature of all in the sea is...

ALAIN GRÉE

For more on Button Books, contact:

GMC Publications Ltd
Castle Place, 166 High Street, Lewes, East Sussex, BN7 1XU
United Kingdom
Tel +44 (0)1273 488005
www.gmcbooks.com